Viewing an American Ethnic Community

Rochester, New York, Italians in Photographs

Frank A. Salamone

UNIVERSITY PRESS OF AMERICA,® INC.
Lanham • Boulder • New York • Toronto • Plymouth, UK

Copyright © 2010 by
University Press of America,® Inc.
4501 Forbes Boulevard
Suite 200
Lanham, Maryland 20706
UPA Acquisitions Department (301) 459-3366

Estover Road
Plymouth PL6 7PY
United Kingdom

Library of Congress Control Number: 2009936880
ISBN: 978-0-7618-4814-1 (paperback : alk. paper)
eISBN: 978-0-7618-4815-8

This work is dedicated to many people. First, is my wife Virginia who encouraged me to put together a book showing the Italian community in Rochester, NY, in its many various activities. It is also dedicated to my parents, Angelo and Frances, who taught me to be Italian and American. My sister has been a large part of my life as have my children, grandchildren, great-grandchild, cousins, and friends. If a city can be a character in one's story, then Rochester, NY, is a major one in mine. People not from Rochester cannot grasp its importance in the memories of those who have come from there. To all, thanks for all you have given me in my life.

There is no end. There is no beginning. There is only the infinite passion of life

—Federico Fellini

Contents

Preface

NINETY-THREE YEARS YOUNG: JOSEPH LO CURTO

On January 9, 2008, a rare spring like day in the midst of Rochester's arctic winter, my friend of over 50 years, Sib Petix, and I interviewed his uncle Joseph Lo Curto. Lo Curto is a young and vigorous 93 years old. For many years, he has been a pillar of the Italian community, working tirelessly for the promotion of Italian culture and language. At the same time, he was a successful businessman, along with his two brothers.

Among his many accomplishments was the founding of the Casa Italiana at Nazareth College. As with so many other projects, the Casa took a great deal of persuading and the familiar mantra of lack of equipment, teachers, students, books and anything else of need was heard. However, Lo Curto with the help of others, mainly his nephew Sib Petix, managed to collect $206, 000 for the Casa. In 1977 the Casa opened with no debt, a new building, complete with furniture and books. It has thrived over the years, presenting many programs to the general public and encouraging Italian language programs in the community.

The Casa was but one of many of Lo Curto's accomplishments in the community. He has worked hard to get the Italian language taught in the public and Catholic schools of Rochester. His efforts began in the 1940s when he first approached Rochester's Board of Education to provide Italian language instruction to Rochester's children. In response to the Board's statement that no one wanted Italian in the schools and that there were no demands for it, Lo Curto presented a petition to the Board with over 1,000 signatures, asking that their children be given the opportunity to study Italian. In time, East High School and Franklin High taught Italian. Other schools followed, including a number of Catholic schools, such as Aquinas, Nazareth Academy, and McQuaid Jesuit High School.

Lo Curto led by example; for 25 years he taught evening school at Eastridge High School in the Rochester suburb of Irondequoit. His classes in conversational Italian introduced many to the glories of Italian culture, including its great writers like Dante, Tasso, and others, as well as its music and art. Lo Curto put his university education to good use in helping educate his fellow-Italians as well as the general community.

For many years he and his wife were active in promoting opera in Rochester. They helped found and promote the Rochester Opera Company, now the Mercury Opera. Major stars were hired to perform in operas in which local people filled the chorus and minor roles. The opera performed at the Eastman Theater and the Auditorium, major venues in a city known for its cultural life.

Lo Curto was involved with many other projects over the years. He was a major force in founding the Italian Cultural Society and Il Solco. These organizations met monthly and discussed topics of interest to those involved in Italian culture. Often professors from one of Rochester's schools of higher learning would speak to the group. Art, music, literature and general cultural material would be the topics of conversation. Many teachers attended these meetings and helped spread the word in their classrooms about Italian culture.

Although Lo Curto states that he encountered no open prejudice in his business or personal life, prejudice was always present below the surface. His work helped present a positive image of Italians to counteract negative stereotypes found in newspapers, radio, and the mass media in general. It was a quiet, persistent, and fruitful work, one which helped change people's minds about the mainly poor and blue-collar southern Italian immigrants who populated Rochester. Times changed for the better and it was the efforts of people like Joseph Lo Curto, which helped them change.

Acknowledgments

There are many people who assisted this work. The Rochester Public Library, The Rochester Museum and Science Center, The City of Rochester Photography Center, Sister of Saint Joseph Archives, Josephine Costanza (my sister), my cousins, son, and other relatives who shared photos, various people who consented to interviews, Joe Lo Curto, St. John Fisher College Library and Alumni Center, The Catholic Courier Journal, Sr. Connie Derby and the Catholic Archives, and so many other people. To all—thanks from the bottom of my heart. And thanks to the good Sisters of St. Joseph at their archives for their prayers when I was operated on. They worked.

Introduction

I have long been interested in the ethnography and history of Rochester's Italians. After all, self-knowledge is the beginning of wisdom and Lord knows I could use wisdom. I knew that to know myself I had to know from whence I came. That meant I had to come to grips with my background in Rochester, New York, and the people among whom I grew up.

I had had a happy childhood, filled with loving relatives and parents who obviously cared for my sister and me. They were fortunate enough to have siblings who gladly supplied additional love to us. There were many cousins to provide companionship and additional insights on the mysteries of life. And noise—joyous noise! We were a large, noisy group, who were taught to express our views on life with absolute conviction even when, and especially when, we were not sure of them.

My mother was a large part of that group and my life. She was always in my corner but not always sure of what I was doing. She did not know why I had to go to Nigeria to do my research, or really what that research was. So, I decided to do some research on a topic of interest to her, Italians in Rochester. I interviewed her, her sisters, my father's siblings, cousins, and various other people in Rochester. I went to archives, churches, and various other sites. She began to get a feel for what I did and why. It fit the Italian character.

Curiosity is part of the cultures. Some might term it nosiness. We want to know what is going on and why. We need to know where the power may be and we are skeptical of easy explanations. People's motives are always suspect and our own often hidden. My mother could get on board with that viewpoint—and did. Along the way, I learned much about my own background. There were explanations about things which I had always wondered. Relationships became clearer to me. In understanding these things, I began to understand myself better.

Maybe the world is not really divided into those who are Italian and those who want to be. However, there has always been a great deal of interest in Italian culture. I am showing the best of that culture in this book. Let others point out our shortcomings. We know what they are. But I wish to point out the joy of being there among the people who brought Italian sausage and lasagna to picnics while others ate hot dogs. We did not feel ashamed or strange. We felt we were trail blazers in the art of enjoying life.

And we still do!

Chapter One

Immigration

The first Italian settlers in Rochester faced problems common to immigrants elsewhere. Basically, they were outsiders and, contrary to the myth that Italians were welcomed in America before the large immigration of the latter nineteenth century, were made to feel that hostility from earlier settlers. Although there were agencies that did social welfare work among the immigrants and were accepted by them, most notably The Practical Housekeeping Center, later known as Lewis Street Center, and the Practical Nursing Association, the Italian immigrants became noted for their desire to solve their own problems and to pay their own bills. The instrument that enabled them to do so was the society or voluntary association.

Interestingly, although many of these associations were based on *campagnia* or *regione,* such as the *Caltanisetta* or *Vulgarnara* Societies, very quickly they served to present a united Italian ethnic identity. Even the use of regions united villages which otherwise were distinct in "the Old Country." It is an irony not often appreciated that Calabrians, Sicilians, and others had to come to America to become Italians. A significant part of that transformation occurred in clubs as a necessary response to prejudice and discrimination in the Rochester environment.

The local Gannet papers attitude toward Italians has been noted above. It continued to treat Italians as either quaint or dangerous depending on the circulation needs of the moment. An interesting example is its illustrated article on the description of immigrants in Rochester (*Union & Advertiser*, Jan. 31, 1889, 3–2).

The house depicted as a typical "Arcadian" dwelling is, in reality, a summer house used by people to do some farming in a section they termed "le lotte" (the lots) and to get some fresh air. The purpose of the article was to stress the alien

1

and inscrutable nature of Italians, a nature so different it would bar them from participating equally in Rochester's society. Therefore, it is understandable that the immigrants pushed to emphasize their willingness to become Americans. At the same time they began to underscore Italian contributions to western civilization from which American values ultimately sprang.

Courtesy Josephine Costanza. Chain migration was a means used to bring relatives to Rochester. In this case, the middle son brought his brothers to Rochester, NY. He also brought his father and mother and numerous other relatives to America. Although men generally came to America first, those who stayed tended to bring their family members to America quickly. As the gentleman in the middle often stated in reply to how beautiful Sicily was, "You can't eat beauty!"

Courtesy Rochester Museum and Science Center Strong Collection. Many Italian immigrants attended classes first to become citizens and second to advance their prospects in America. These brothers appear ready to tackle the task successfully.1.3.

Courtesy Rochester Museum and Science Center Strong Collection. Italians participated in the Rochester Centennial Celebration in 1918. They were never shy about sharing their culture with their fellow Rochesterians. They saw this as a way of combating negative stereotypes, which circulated quite freely about them.

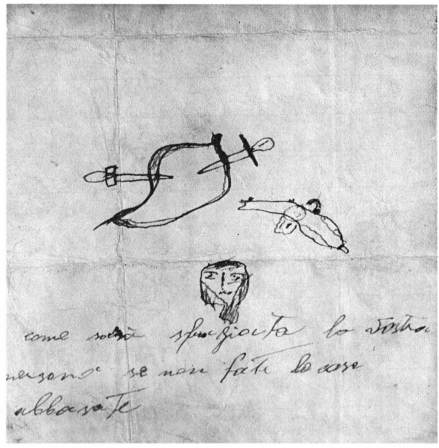

Courtesy of the Rochester Museum and Science Center. This is a warning note from the Black Hand, the predecessor of the Mafia. Unfortunately many immigrants took advantage of their fellow immigrants. The Black Hand was the most egregious of those, like unscrupulous landlords or padrone, who exploited honest, hardworking family men.

Casa Italiana, "Apice" of His Dream

By PATTY MACK

Joseph J. LoCurto has a dream. He wants to establish a means by which the local Italian-American community can share its rich cultural background with other Rochesterians.

Fulfilling that dream hasn't been easy.

It took years to convince area high schools to add Italian-language classes to their curriculums.

Colleges and universities throughout the country have only recently expanded their foreign studies programs to include Italian courses.

Even interest by third and fourth generation Italian-Americans in their heritage hasn't always been all that great.

But now with enrollment in Italian language classes on the rise across the nation, with several American colleges offering Italian as a major course of study, and with a renewed interest in Italy and her culture on the part of younger members of the Italian-American community, all that is changing.

As a result LoCurto will see his dream fulfilled with the establishment of Casa Italiana, a center for the study of Italian language, culture, history, and art at Nazareth College.

LoCurto, who is president of New Crown Beverages, has been a longtime supporter of Italian-American cultural events in Rochester.

He came up with the idea of building a "casa Italiana" in January while helping plan for the Italian Festival which is being held at Nazareth this week.

THIS CENTER, he told Nazareth officials, could be a gift from the Italian-American community to the college.

So with the help of two other area businessmen — Joseph P. Gagliano, president of Mike and Joe Equipment Co., Inc., and Joseph Mancini, president of Monroe Forgings Division of Amtel Metals Corp. — he started making plans to raise the $100,000 needed to get the center underway.

Fund raising efforts begin tomorrow with a $15 a head benefit gala slated to begin at the Nazareth Arts Center at 8 p.m.

The events will include an Italian folk dancing exhibition, poetry reading, piano recital, Italian travelogues, entertainment by strolling troubadours, and dancing to the music of the Five-O group, and champagne reception. Reservations can be made by calling 586-2525.

Plans for the "Casa Italiana," which are being drawn up by local architect Michael DeAngelis, are sketchy at this point, LoCurto said.

It will resemble a Renaissance-style Italian villa. And it may include an outdoor area where dance, theatrical, and musical performances can be held.

LoCurto said the center will have a library, reading room, small auditorium, seminar rooms, reception rooms, and kitchen facilities.

Future plans may call for the addition of residential quarters.

Columbus University is the only other American College to have a "casa Italiana,"

LoCurto said. Nazareth will work closely with Columbia's language department in planning their facility.

LoCurto said Nazareth will have sole responsibility for the programs to be held in the center.

Dr. Virginia Ott, head of the college's foreign language department, said those programs may include Italian film festivals, industrial and art exhibits, lectures, discussion groups, seminars, and adult education courses in Italian art, music, economics, and language.

The center will also house the Italian section of the college's foreign language department, she said. It may serve as an office for a visiting professor from Italy. And it will most likely spur growth in Nazareth's Italian studies program, she said.

Construction will begin as soon as money is available, LoCurto said.

In the meantime, Italian programs will get underway next September in a Nazareth classroom building.

LoCurto said Casa I' will add "attenti

Italian community and focus attention on Nazareth and on Rochester.

"We have a rich heritage of culture and we felt it should be diffused more than it has been in the past," he said.

"We have reached a climax, the 'apice' (let's put it in Italian) of a dream."

Joseph Lo Curto Files. Joe was instrumental in aiding the foundation of a Casa Italiana in Rochester, NY. He helped raise money for the project and promoted it tirelessly.

Albert R. Stone Negative Collection, Rochester Museum & Science Center 1920.
"James Angelo and Angelina Mancuso rehearse the tarantella, an Italian folk dance,
to be performed at the Homelands Exhibition of 1920 held at Exposition Park. The
Homelands Exhibition was an ethnic festival celebrating the contributions of immigrants
who had come to Rochester from other countries. The Homelands Exhibition in 1920
was organized in the aftermath of the "red scare" of the post World War I years, which
triggered much anti-foreigner sentiment. The Chamber of Commerce learned, in 1919, of
a homelands exhibit in Chicago, and sponsored one in Rochester, with the cooperation
of the Memorial Art Gallery, the Board of Education, the city administration and others.
A 10-day Homelands Exhibition was staged at Exposition Park in April, 1920. More
than 200 people of 17 nationalities prepared 24 booths, dramatic and musical numbers
for each nationality, and enlisted 2000+ participants in the performances. The exhibits
included art objects, costumes, and furniture brought by immigrant families from their
homelands. The exhibit served to create interest in and respect for immigrant art, culture
and traditions among the general population. It also reassured 2d and 3d generation
Americans of the value of their heritage. The Homelands Exhibition was repeated in
1928, and at several times in the 1940s and 1950, often at the Memorial Art Gallery."

Rochester Public Library Local History Division picture file. "Samuel Moulthrop, noted Rochester educator, teaching a citizenship class at Washington Grammar School. Citizenship classes focused on language and other skills."

Minnie, Charles, Connie (Babe), and Jacob Salamone.

Chapter Two

Community

Ruth Keene's 1946 Sociological Master's Thesis provides a glimpse into the status of Rochester's Italians in 1940. It also demonstrates the bias, which Italians still had to overcome in the following years. Keene points out that the percentage of the foreign born in Rochester had declined from 12.7% of the population to 9.7%. She innocently concludes that never again would people have to worry about the growth of immigration. Moreover, the median age of the foreign born population, mainly Italian in Rochester, was 50.9. However, she (1946: IV) notes ". . . the children of the foreign-born have just reached the productive phase of their lives. During the next twenty years our concerns will be with these persons who are themselves in a particular phase of the acculturation process. They are in a peculiar middle position, experiencing and learning the ways of the country of their parents at home, but meeting the impact of the American culture at school, in their jobs, and in their community contacts."

To Keene and other concerned Rochesterians this issue of "acculturation" was of primary importance. From their point of view, 17.8% of Rochester's population, 56, 329 people according to the 1940 census, was of Italian origin. It was not simply that there were 56,329 "Italians," born in Italy or America, out of 324,975 people but according to Keene (5-6) these Italians were a high welfare people. Moreover, they have a high delinquency rate, over two times that of other American children. She points out they "live in last chance areas," with overcrowding. Their unemployment rates are greater than other Rochesterians. Needless to say, their status was low. She concludes finally that there is a need to understand Italian culture to solve the problem.

Keene went on, however, to note that Italians had not yet been assimilated. Moreover, she understood that there was not a single homogeneous American

Italian culture, a point too often overlooked in writings about Italian Americans. It is also important to note that a large number of Italians left America and returned to Italy. Indeed in the 1920s more Italians left to return to Italy than came to America. Many, in fact, did come to America with the explicit idea of staying for a short time and, contrary to many myths that have arisen, did just that. 62.8% of all Italians who came from Italy returned. When one considers that young men who came without their families made up the majority of those coming to America and that there were 135.8 males for every 100 females up to and including the 1940 Rochester census, it is not surprising that so many people returned. It also suggests that those Italians who remained in the United States differed from those who did not.

They followed the typical pattern of settling in areas with other immigrants of their own group. In 1940, for example, 6.092 Italians, 29.1 percent, of their total population were living in but six census tracts. Over 50% of Italians in Rochester were in thirteen census tracts, according to Keene (p. 50). By 1940, however, there was some movement out of these areas, a movement that accelerated greatly by 1960. Moreover, Keene reported changes among children of Italian immigrants, which foreshadowed even greater changes ahead.

Italians in Rochester had to adapt to the overall situation in Rochester. Rochester's population was 324,975, a slight drop from the 1930 census. It was the first drop in its history. However, Rochester remained the twenty-third largest city in the United States, the same position it held in 1930. Additionally, Rochester was a city of home owners and Keene presents evidence that Italian immigrants and their children were moving into their own homes. Despite the bleak picture with which she opens her thesis, Keene does conclude that the first generation born in the United States was being "acculturated" into Rochester's society. And what was that society like in 1940?

From its founding in 1803 by Colonel Nathaniel Rochester, for whom the city is named, to 1845, the city grew to 25,000 people, 30% of whom were foreign born. McKelvey writes that 1845 was the first year in which a foreign census was taken (McKelvey 1963: 1). In the 1870s the percentage of the foreign born and their children reach 70% and remained at that level until its decline in the 1920s, despite a large influx of Puerto Ricans after World War II and refugees from Eastern Europe and elsewhere in the same period.

Italians had to adapt to this ethnic mix and did so more easily that Keene, for example, has noted. The predominant or ruling culture and cultural group in Rochester was the Anglo-Saxon or WASP contingent. Irish and Germans, Catholic or not, were de facto members of the group. There was not one simple process of "acculturation" going on. There were a number of adaptations being made. First, Italians had to form a somewhat homogenous group out of a very heterogeneous mix of people, mainly but not totally from Southern

Italy and Sicily. This group had to be able to assert its claims to political and economic rights. This group formation was not always easy since the concept of a united Italy and its actual creation did not come about until 1871. Many immigrants had but a vague idea of that entity and were more tied to their villages and regions than to the country of Italy.

Then there was the process of adapting to and coming to grips with the dominant WASP culture. The old "English" ruling class still had great power in Rochester. While there was a spirit of noblesse oblige, which fueled great charities, there was also a feeling of being condescended to on the part of the Italians. The English, moreover, made various alliances with earlier ethnic groups to control local politics. Additionally, there were other ethnic groups in Rochester, which had to be taken into account.

Even other Catholic ethnic groups posed problems. The Rochester Catholic Church, as in so many other places, was controlled by the Irish. Even German Catholics did not want Italians bringing their "pagan" rites into their churches. The creation of National Parishes helped ease some of the problems as did the appointed, as I noted, of pastors who spoke Italian and who had sympathy for the culture and idiosyncrasies of the people. By 1940 Italian-American young men were becoming priests and taking their places in the parishes.

Meanwhile Italians forged ties with Poles who were also outsiders in ways similar to those of Italians. That did not mean that Italian-Americans remained strictly to themselves. There were warm ties with Jews who often lived in the same neighborhoods and were also victims of discrimination, frequently more violent than that Italians and Italian-Americans faced. Those Italians who were musically inclined, especially in the younger generation, also formed ties with African Americans, as did Gap and Chuck Mangione, for example, just as their uncle Jerre Mangione forged close ties with Jews with whom people frequently mistook him, as he notes in many places.

However, for those of us growing up in the 1940s and 50s there was one major distinction; namely, that between Italians and Americans. All other distinctions, within the Italian community or the American one, were subsidiary to this one big dichotomy. I can remember resisting the dichotomy even as I also embraced it unconsciously. The suspicion of others that Ann Parson (1969 and 1966) notes of Italians and the turning to the family in times of trouble since it is the center of their universe were also powerful unconscious forces. However, many of those who "came up" in the forties and fifties branched out away from the tried and true and made close friends across ethnic lines without losing their ethnic sense, but a sense shaped by the changing world of that period.

The Second World War was a major factor in changing the lives of Americans. It changed those of young and old and yet to come. Although Rochester lost population in 1940 for the first time in its history, it was still the twenty-third largest city in the United States. As the war approached Rochester's economy recovered from the Great Depression. Its industry and surrounding farms supported the war effort at home and overseas. The prosperity that came with World War II lasted throughout the fifties and into the sixties.

It also led to a movement into the suburbs. The 1950 census marked a growth of the city of Rochester to its highest level, about 333,000. However the 1960s census showed that people in Rochester, as throughout the country, were moving to the suburbs. The closest suburbs, of course, were first to surge in population. Greece, Gates, Chili, Henrietta, Brighton and Irond-equoit demonstrated growth and had all the problems associated with it. The 1960 census showed a drop in Rochester's population to 318,611. Even worse for its boosters, Rochester dropped to 38th in rank of American cities. These changes brought about alterations in almost every aspect of people's lives, including the lives of Italian-Americans.

Davis St. area after urban renewal. Davis St. was a center of Italian east side settlement. Rochester City Photos Archives.

Two immigrants at Rochester Public Market. Rochester City Photos Archives.

Personal Photo. Law School graduation puts another professional in the world that just might help the family in the future. Frank C. Salamone and a friend at Hofstra Law School Graduation, 2008.

Mark, Stephen, and David Salamone in top photo. Frank Salamone at college graduation.

Personal Photo. An oldest son and youngest grandchild make a fine combination. Mark and Jonathan Salamone.

Joe Lo Curto and nephew Sib Petix. Courtesy of Joseph Lo Curto.

Veltre Bakery. Rochester City Archives.

Scio Street.

War relief efforts for WWII.

Chapter Three

Family

The term "family" could mean many things, depending on how wanted to use it, for inclusion or exclusion. The core, of course, is the nuclear family. Beyond that were so many relatives, grandparents, aunts and uncles, cousins of all degrees and just friends who were fictive kin; that is, honorific family. In many families there were often overlapping ties, which only family members could figure out. We were related to many relatives on both sides of the family, allied to others in various ways, some of which I still need to consult others on. Indeed, family events often exposed alliances and fault lines in the family. There were also lines of seniority and genuine friendship along the way. Some siblings were closer to each other than they were to others as were some cousins. These alliance could change frequently, and, as I observed, with lightning swiftness.

People dropped in on you all the time. Sometimes a phone call might announce your coming or even an invitation. However, relatives and neighbors or just plain friends stopped by. Thus, the house was always spotless and God help you if you didn't do your chores. Since most women were working in our family that meant we kids had to do our share of the two or three times a week cleaning of the entire house. No dishes, of course, were left to dry on their own and none left to soak in the sink. No baseboard went unpolished for more than a few days. Dust was the enemy. Our parents were all too aware of the slurs "Americans" mouthed about "dirty Italians."

There were many customary celebrations, of course. First Communions, Confirmations, anniversaries, and birthdays were holidays and even when we were too old to have all the relatives over and wanted just our friends, the relatives showed up. So we split our time between the two groups, hoping to break away from one group to go to the outside world but always feeling the tug back into the security of the family. Roots continued to anchor us, whether we wished them to do so or not.

Personal Photo. Angelo Salamone, Frances Polvino Salamone and Wedding Party. September 25, 1930. Wedding celebrations could go on for two or three days.

Giacomo Camillari. An early labor leader in Rochester.

Papa Frank Salamone and nephew.

Grandma Angelina Polvino and daughters, Frances and Antoinette.

Grandma Angelina Polvino and daughters, Antoinette, Jenny, and Frances.

Marion Salamone, High School Graduation.

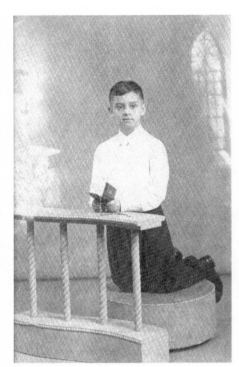

Frank Salamone, Confirmation Day.

Mama Frances Salamone in her youth.

Josephine Salamone, my sister, at about 6 months. Family events were always cause for celebration. Babies tend to be the center of celebration. Babies, such as Jo Salamone, were the apple of their parents' eyes. Weddings called the whole family together. Marion Salamone was happy to be her cousin's maiden of honor. Graduation was always a big occasion, another excuse for a party to reaffirm family ties and celebrate life itself.

Extended families were important to Italian Americans but nuclear families were the building blocks. Jacob, Ida, Jacqueline, and Jean Salamone. Courtesy of Steve Imburgia.

Lo Curto family. The family has been very successful in Rochester. Joe was a founder of businesses in the area, a teacher, and a founder of the Casa Italiana. Photo is one celebrating the opening of New Crown beverages on North Street.

Joseph Lo Curto and his sister Mary.

Ida Sabatini and Jake Salamone Wedding.

St. John Fisher Graduation 1961.

Two Concettas, Lo Curto and Petix.

Personal Photo. Angelo Salamone, Mark, and Stephen.

Angelo Salamone and Frances Polvino Wedding September, 1930. Sometimes it seemed that the purpose of life was to have grandchildren. They were proof that one would live on in the next generation. Family events are celebrated. Graduations are signs of success. One's life meant something and would carry on into the future.

Chapter Four

Work

In the 1920s there were 21,000 Italians in Rochester. There were Italians in a number of jobs—500 grocers, 200 barbers, 600 or more in public utilities and in freight car yards. There were others in parts manufacturing and cigar making, among various miscellaneous jobs. However, the largest number of Italian workers, more than 4500, worked in the clothing industry while another 2500 or so worked in shoe manufacturing. Into the 1970s around 80% of Hickey-Freeman's clothing workers were of Italian origin. The unionization of the clothing industry was central to their role in American life. (Democrat & Chronicle May 30: 1976).

Eastman Kodak, on the other hand, generally employed few Italians. The general feeling in Rochester among Italians is that this fact was a firm Kodak policy. The few Italians who worked for Kodak tended to be those who did not have Italian names and who did not look Italian. Specifically, they tended to have light hair and light skin. Blue eyes were also an aid. Part of the desire to keep Italians out went along with Kodak's anti-union bias and its embrace of the alternate system of Welfare Capitalism. Immigrants and their children appeared to be too pro-union, possibly even pro-socialist.

Interestingly, as the clothing industry all but died in Rochester after the 1960s, Kodak began employing more Italians and other ethnics. The fear of unions had diminished as union membership also diminished. My childhood best friend found employment in Kodak without altering his name. His light skin and hair didn't hurt but he did not have to change his very Italian last name, Bonfiglio or his given name, Mario. Times were changing in the sixties!

Courtesy Rochester Museum and Science Center Strong Collection – Rochester Women were active in union work. The myth of the meek Italian wife was perpetuated by those who did not know Italian women. Italian women were strong and quick to assert their rights. They were active in labor causes and a bulwark of the Amalgamated Clothing Workers of America.

Michael Sterns Factory. Courtesy Gannett Papers.

Factory in the 1930s and 1940s.

Factory in the 1930s and 1940s.

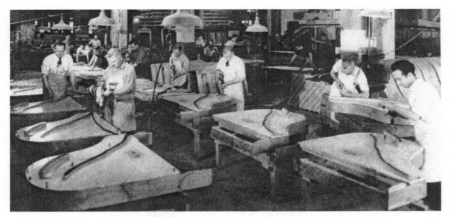

Factory in the 1930s and 1940s.

Factory in the 1930s and 1940s.

Factory in the 1930s and 1940s.

Factory in the 1930s and 1940s.

Lyell Avenue and Train Tracks.

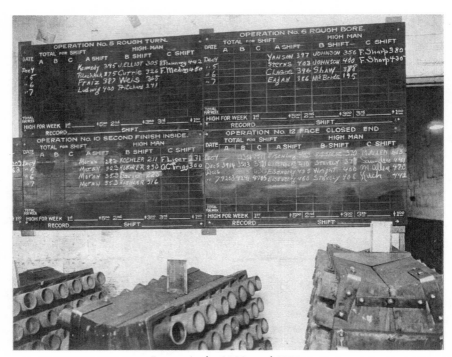

Factory in the 1930s and 1940s.

Many Italians owned their own small businesses. This is Patsy Sabatini in his store. Courtesy Steve Imburgia.

Chapter Five

Religion

Religion, as a cultural artifact, is more than a system for arranging people in groups to address the supernatural and perform appropriate rituals. It is a boundary marker, useful as a means for political mobilization and self/other identification. It can, in other words, be used as a symbolic means for arranging people in groups to address political and economic issues vital to their perceived interests. It can become a master identity.

Immigrants fueled the growth of the Catholic Church in Rochester. The Italians become the largest of these immigrant groups. The policy of Rochester's first Bishop, Bishop McQuaid, was to find priests for each of the ethnic groups who spoke the language of the people, and, if possible came from that group. McQuaid fostered the growth of national parishes, founding new parishes as the situation demanded. It was his goal not to let parishes become too large to defeat their familial nature

In addition, McQuaid desired the establishment of Catholic schools to combat the sectarianism of the public schools. His initial goal was to obtain tax money for the support of these schools. However, failing that he moved for parochial schools, supported by the diocese and parish, staffed with teaching sisters. McQuaid believed that children learn their religion in schools. Along with the three "r"s, there was a fourth, religion. So he ordered, "Build schoolhouses then for the religious education of your children as the best protest against a system of education from which religion has been excluded by law."

The Sisters of St. Joseph were employed in the Rochester Diocese to work with Rochester's youngsters, especially Italians. The objective was to keep them away from Protestant influence and attempts to convert them. There were, of course, other congregations of nuns who taught in the schools. I was taught by the School Sisters of Notre Dame. It seemed as if every church had a school or was planning to build one. Schools not only served to preserve the faith, they also provided a means for social events to bind the congregation together.

Catholic Courier Journal's Article on Recreation Center. With permission.

St. Francis Xavier's Catholic Schoolgirls. Catholic Courier Journal. With permission.

Father Moffat, pastor of St. Francis, turning first spade of dirt for new church. Catholic Courier Journal. With permission.

St. Lucy's Church. Catholic Courier Journal. With permission.

Growth at St. Lucy's Parish

after the death of Fr. Catalano, and served until 1954. The present Convent was purchased in 1913 when Sr. M. Hilary was principal.

Upon the death of Msgr. Maselli in 1954, Rev. Francis Christantielli became the third pastor of St. Lucy's to serve until his death in 1956. Rev. Gennaro Ventura was appointed as Administrator and is still serving in that capacity.

In reviewing the 44 years of its existence, nostalgic memories must come back to many. Three generations have found, in St. Lucy's, a spiritual fortress where the lives of thousands have been intertwined with the life of the parish. The priests of St. Lucy's have, for 44 years, been with

her loved ones when they threw off the shadows of this life to enter the shadowless light of the Presence of God.

Thousands have learned the eternal truths of their religion under the self-sacrificing and selfless nuns who live only for God. Through the years, the Eucharistic Christ has been placed on the tongues of the faithful six or seven hundred thousand times with the age-old formula, "May the Body of Our Lord Jesus Christ keep your soul unto life everlasting. Amen."

St. Lucy's Parish has spiritually fed her children for 44 years. She has joined them in marriage, she has forgiven them their sins. She has been concerned with her children. She has striven to make them solicitous concerning treasures that grow not old — treasures in Heaven that fail not.

What will be the story of the next 50 years at St. Lucy's? It depends on the faith and loyalty and generosity of each of her sons and daughters of today. Just as your parents and grandparents did not fail you, neither will you fail your children and their children's children.

Article on St. Lucy's parish, another Italian parish on the West Side. Catholic Courier Journal. With permission.

Forty-four Years of Spi...

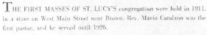

celebrated. The school was opened to children in the fall of 1913, the nuns residing at St. Mary's Orphan Asylum and St. Patrick's Girl's Asylum.

In 1919 there was a registration of 394 pupils under the guidance of Sr. M. Bertrand who was principal for 14 years.

Members of the 1918 class, the first to graduate from St. Lucy's were: Anna Belardino, Florence D'Argento, Philippine Mendetcole, and Anna Palermo. Classes for public school students were also conducted by the Sisters of St. Joseph at St. Lucy's.

Msgr. Benedict Maselli became the second pastor of St. Lucy's in 1926

THE FIRST MASSES OF ST. LUCY'S congregation were held in 1911 in a store on West Main Street near Brown. Rev. Mario Catalano was the first pastor, and he served until 1926.

In 1912 the holy sacrifice of the Mass was celebrated in SS. Peter and Paul's Convent on King Street when that congregation moved to their present church on West Main Street. At this time, under Fr. Catalano's direction, and assisted by Fiore Barbato, Gennaro Mangini, and Liberato Spina, the present St. Lucy's Church and School was being built. The windows and bricks from the old SS. Peter and Paul Church were used in the present edifice.

The Sisters of St. Joseph began their missionary work in the parish at this time — assembling the children to attend the 10:30 daily Mass.

With the additional help of Anthony Barbato, Anthony Tardello, Joseph Cantabella, Louis Astone, Vincenzio Muscatella, construction of the Church and School was completed in 1913, consecrated and the first Mass

Article on St. Lucy's parish, another Italian parish on the West Side. Catholic Courier Journal. With permission.

The Catholic Rosary for Peace was broadcast from St. Francis of Assisi Parish. Catholic Courier Journal. With permission.

Radio rosary show is back

Msgr. Cirrincione can be heard on 1460-AM

Mike Latona/Catholic Courier

Accompanied by some revisions, the long-running Family Rosary for Peace has returned to early-evening radio after a two-week hiatus.

The show went back on the air July 16 on Rochester's WHIC 1460-AM, formerly Christian-format WWWG. It is being broadcast four evenings per week with an air time of 7 p.m., slightly later than its former slot of 6:30.

Although tapes of the late Msgr. Joseph Cirrincione's program have continued airing seven days per week on two other Rochester stations — 9:30 p.m. on WLGZ 990-AM and 5 a.m. on WDCZ 102.7-FM — followers of the show apparently felt a void in the early evening, where Family Rosary for Peace has run continuously since its inception in 1950.

"A lot of listeners had called and contacted us, saying 'I miss Msgr. Cirrincione.' We certainly took those comments into serious consideration," said William Purcell, general manager of Buffalo's Holy Family Communications, which acquired WHIC on July 1. "Catholic devotions are important to us, and obviously a tradition with such local impact is something important to continue."

"Many people were calling us and the diocese," added Father Paul Tomasso, director of Family Rosary for Peace. "We're very happy that it's back. We're working with (WHIC) in order to continue it as the great tradition it is."

Family Rosary for Peace had previously aired seven days per week on WWWG but is only running on Monday, Tuesday, Wednesday and Friday on WHIC. However, Purcell emphasized that WHIC — the first all-Catholic radio station in Rochester — has greatly increased the overall offering of rosaries on 1460-AM. Nationally produced rosaries air seven days per week at 11 a.m., as well as Monday through Friday at 10:30 a.m. The Thursday 7 p.m. slot features a Buffalo-based rosary show with the Luminous Mysteries.

Purcell said copies of the Family Rosary for Peace have been edited for better quality and transferred from audio to compact disc to enhance preservation. Unfortunately, Purcell said, evening prayer by Msgr. Cirrincione that followed the

File photo

Msgr. Joseph Cirrincione, founder of the Family Rosary for Peace, leads an early broadcast on radio station WSAY. After a two-week hiatus, the long-running show is back on the air on Rochester's first all-Catholic radio station, WHIC 1460-AM.

rosaries are in such poor shape that they're being replaced on the WHIC broadcasts by different prayers.

The time switch on WHIC from 6:30 to 7 p.m., Purcell explained, is due to a time conflict with Catholic Answers, a live syndicated call-in show that runs from 6 to 7 p.m. that is Holy Family Communications' most popular program.

Family Rosary for Peace has aired on 1460-AM since 1979, when WWWG acquired the program following a 29-year run on WSAY 1240-AM. WSAY and WWWG have served as the program's flagship stations; many other radio outlets across the Rochester Diocese have also carried the show in the past. In recent years tapes of the show were run after Msgr. Cirrincione's failing

health prevented him from doing live broadcasts. Msgr. Cirrincione, who died in November 2002, served as the show's director from its founding until 1998, when Father Tomasso became director.

WHIC, a 5,000-watt station, offers national Catholic programs, devotionals and Masses. Locally generated programming is also expected to increase as the station takes root. Purcell said station management has, thus far, received "tremendously positive feedback from the community — a number of phone calls and e-mails. People are truly glad to have Catholic radio in Rochester."

Purcell invites listener feedback by calling 877/888-6279, or e-mailing info@holyfamily.ws.

News & Analysis Catholic Courier | Diocese of Rochester, NY | July 24, 2003

Article celebrating anniversary of St. Lucy's parish. Catholic Courier Journal. With permission.

St. Michael's Church tower. Rochester archives. With permission.

St. Michael's Church tower. Rochester archives. With permission.

Rochester Catholic parish.

Rochester Catholic parish.

Rochester Catholic parish.

HALL

SCHOOL

Rochester Catholic parish.

Rochester Catholic parish.

Rochester Catholic parish.

Photos from St. John Fisher, courtesy of St. John Fisher.

How Fisher students dressed in the 1950s.

Bishop James Kearney at St. John Fisher College. With permission of St. John Fisher College.

Student Dances at Fisher.

Student Dances at Fisher.

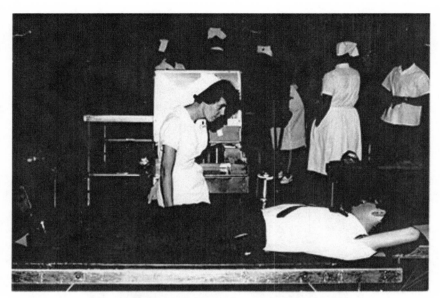

Nurse with Fisher student, giving blood.

Sisters of St. Joseph. The Sisters had a special vocation to teach Italian children in Rochester.

Holy Redeemer Procession in May to crown Mary.

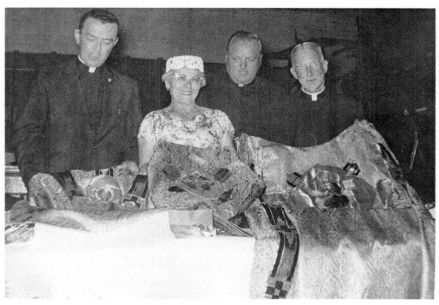

St. Francis Xavier Parish.

St. John Fisher students hard at work in library.

REV. MARIO CATALANO, D.D.

MSGR. BENEDICT MASELLI.

REV. FRANCIS CRISTANTELLI

Parish priests at St. Lucy Parish.

St. Philip Neri. Fr. George Weinman is on the left. He worked all his pastoral life with Italian communities. He was a good friend of mine and died in a Church fire.

Chapter Six

Leisure

Italians in Rochester participated and contributed to Rochester's various leisure activities over the years. From the earliest day, they took part in sports, music of all kinds, theater and literature. Jazz in Rochester, NY, developed within the larger framework of jazz in the United States. Within that larger scene, Italians played a significant role, along with, of course, African Americans, and people of many other cultures. The fact that there are subgenres of jazz is evidence of the very democratic nature of the music itself. It is able to assimilate different elements and styles from different ethnic groups, social classes, and religions and yet maintain its identity in the midst of change. The ever-evolving art that is jazz is capable of fusing various elements into the whole while respecting the uniqueness of each group that contributes to the mix. Enrico Rava, an outstanding Italian jazz trumpet player, notes that you can generally tell an Italian musician from a German, but both are playing jazz. It is part of the democratic genius of jazz that it is able to live up to the motto of the United States "Out of many, one. (E pluribus Unum)."

Rochester was on various entertainment circuits. In the 1950s, for example, it was on the Birdland circuit. My father, for example, took me to see Charlie Ventura at a club when I was just a bit too young to meet the then legal age of 18 to go to a club. Charlie came over and sat with us at the bar. He found a way to communicate with a working man the intricacies of music, while winking at me. He said he often worked into his performance any request, even if it was just for a bar or two. This desire to impress the audience while not unique to Italians is part of the general culture, certainly of the culture of performance.

The 1950s were particularly rich times. As one participant, Noal Cohen puts it, "Since the Eastman School of Music was located in Rochester, the local scene was substantially enriched by many talented Eastman students interested in jazz, even though no jazz studies program existed then. Nonetheless, I can well remember jam sessions held in the tiny Eastman practice rooms with a dozen or so musicians packed in so tightly that there was barely enough air to breathe!"

Thus the local scene which already boasted such budding stars as the Mangione Brothers, bassist Frank Pullara, drummer Roy McCurdy, saxophonists Pee Wee Ellis, Benny Salzano and Joe Romano and others was enhanced and fertilized by Eastman students including bassist Ron Carter, pianists Wolf Knittel and Paul Tardif, saxophonists Larry Combs and Al Regni, and trumpeter Waymon Reed. John Eckert, another fine trumpet player, was also part of this scene although, like me, he was a student at the University of Rochester rather than at Eastman (Noal Cohen's Jazz History Website, http://www.attictoys.com/jazz/index.html)."

There is still a family like feeling among many of the musicians who came up in Rochester. Note the number of Italians, but not only Italians, who came up together and who had contact with the Mangione Brothers, Chuck and Gap. I wrote in a review of Gap's "Stolen Moments" C.D.

A number of world-class musicians have come from Rochester, NY, and nearby towns. Many have passed through the Mangione sphere of influence. Many record with one or both brothers from time to time. Each brother loves to teach and promote fellow musicians. . . "This family-like feeling is felt on "Stolen Moments". The musicians are familiar with each other's work."

However, as Cohen demonstrates on his excellent website, this closeness did not mean that they were insular or isolated. Many great people came through town. A number of them, in fact, found themselves accepting invitations to Mama and Papa Mangione's table for a spaghetti dinner. Frequently, the famous musicians invited local players to join them on the stand. Oscar Peterson did so in a famous jam session as did Dizzy Gillespie on numerous occasions. Cohen has a picture on his site of Peterson's jam in which local musicians joined his trio in performance.

Gap Mangione shared a memory with me.

" . . . about the time when I was still young enough, I had a driver's license but didn't have a car. I had a girlfriend who did have a car. It was a little Renault with a 5-speed transmission. Of course, at the time, those were very unusual. I had such a great time driving it that we tried to find reasons to go and drive somewhere. We heard there was a group playing over near Geneva. Geneva is 50 miles southeast of Rochester and it was kind of outside Geneva. Geneva is a small enough town, outside of Geneva is really the boondocks; this is the night before New Year's Eve about 1958, I think. So we drove down to the place where this jazz group was supposed to be playing. Getting there was like small roads with ruts on either side. And finally, at the end of one road, there was a house, a large house that had the usual beer signs in the window. We went in and there was a fairly large, long bar and there were ay these people who were obviously workers. None of them were in suits, to put it delicately. And they were there for their after-work beer. And in the back, at the end of this bar was some room where they would normally serve sandwiches at noon time for people who might come by. And there was a band playing there and I could see people dancing but I couldn't believe the music I was hearing. So we want into the back room and it was Philly Joe Jones, Paul Chambers, Sonny Clark, and Cannonball Adderley. On an off night in December, there were maybe 30 or 40 people back there, some of them were dancing; that's how I met Cannonball Adderley, That night he asked my brother and I to play and we did. I'm sure that you remember the reason we got the *Jazz* Brothers on record was because we were on the *Cannonball Adderley Presents* series on Riverside. About a year and a half later, we were playing in a club and I got a phone call there in the club from Cannonball asking if we'd be interested in recording for Riverside."

What is true of jazz is true of other art forms and sports. Rochester Italians have been deeply involved in all of them over the years.

The Fashion Park Band Courtesy of Rush Rhees Library University of Rochester.

Lafayette Park 1900.

Highland Park 1910.

Lorenzo's Restaurant.

Ontario Beach Park.

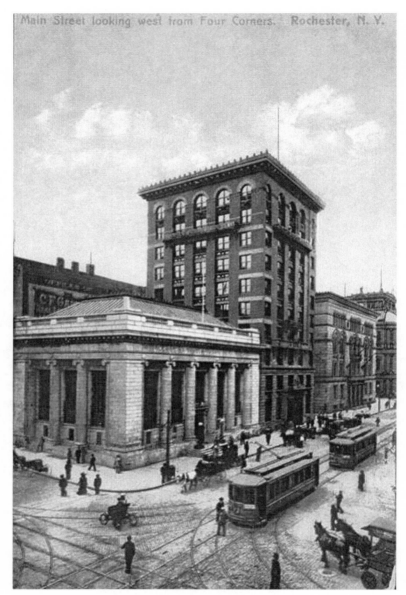

Main Street looking west from Four Corners. Rochester, N. Y.

Main Street West 1910.

Main Street West 1910.

Market Photo. Photo is from Rochester City Archives.

The Tigerettes A woman's social club. Personal photo.

Chuck Mangione and band, brother Gap on piano, at the Mangione home on Cole Street. Noal Cohen's photo archive.

Italian youth at the Centennial Celebration in 1918. Courtesy Stone Collection.

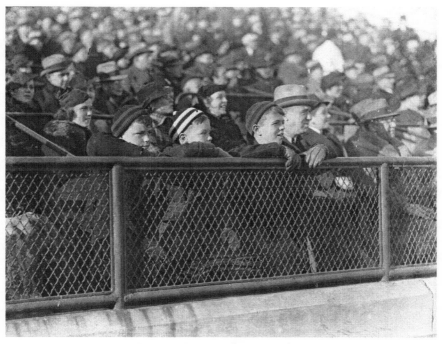

Opening Day at Red Wing Stadium.

Christmas.

Scene of Rochester Celebration. This photo from a free public site.

Opening Day at Red Wing Stadium. Courtesy Rochester Museum and Science Center.

Scene of Rochester Celebration. This photo from a free public site.

Scene of Rochester Celebration. This photo from a free public site.

Scene of Rochester Celebration. This photo from a free public site.

Scene of Rochester Celebration. This photo from a free public site.

Breinigsville, PA USA
18 December 2009
229418BV00002B/5/P